NATIONAL GEOGRAPHIC

Lightning Strikes

PATHFINDER EDITION

By Lesley J. MacDonald

CONTENTS

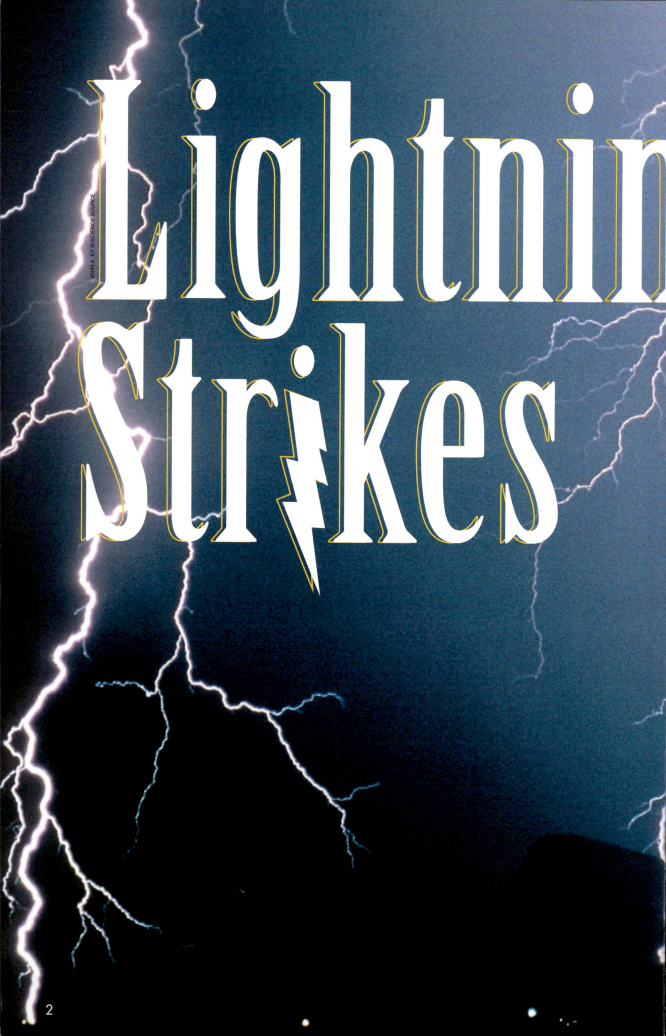

Lightnin

Strikes

By Lesley J. MacDonald

Lightning packs a punch. A single bolt can make more electricity than all the power plants in the United States put together!

Lightning constantly strikes our planet. Every minute nearly 1,800 thunderstorms are brewing somewhere in Earth's sky.

Those storms create about a hundred lightning strikes each second. Many storms make even more. Some large storms generate 425 lightning flashes a minute. During one storm in 1953, more than 600 flashes a minute lit the sky.

Over the years, lightning has done some amazing things. According to one story, lightning struck a house owned by a sword collector in 1891. The sizzling bolt melted the silver on the swords. The molten metal then coated his cat. Every one of the cat's hairs was covered.

Lightning causes many problems too. It starts forest fires and damages buildings. All that destruction adds up. Lightning causes about 139 million dollars of damage yearly. During a year, it also kills some 70 people and injures 300 others.

Sparkling Safety

For years, scientists have been trying to protect people from lightning. Lightning is actually a supercharged bolt of electricity. A protective device has to guide the electricity away from people and buildings.

Benjamin Franklin came up with a way to protect buildings from lightning in the 1750s. That's when he invented the lightning rod. It's a metal rod placed on top of a building. A long wire connects the rod to the ground. When a bolt strikes the rod, the wire carries the electricity safely to the ground.

Not all buildings have lightning rods. So some **meteorologists** want to use rockets to protect people from lightning. A meteorologist is a scientist who studies weather.

Spark of Inspiration. *RIGHT: Benjamin Franklin flew a kite during a thunderstorm in 1752. That helped him prove that lightning is made of electricity. He went on to invent the lightning rod. BELOW: These models helped Franklin develop and test his invention.*

Blast Off to Lightning

Believe it or not, a rocket can be used like a lightning rod. Scientists launch small rockets into storm clouds. Wires attach the rockets to the ground. Lightning strikes the rockets and the wire carries the electricity to the ground.

There are a few problems with the rockets, however. For example, they are expensive. Each one can be used only once. And it is hard to predict where a rocket will fall.

© BETTMANN/CORBIS (FRANKLIN); ERICH LESSING, ART RESOURCE, NY (MODELS)

City Lights. *Lightning zaps the Empire State Building in New York City. A lightning rod at the top keeps the building safe from harm.*

© CLARENCE HOLMES PHOTOGRAPHY/ALAMY

NEW YORKER

Electrifying Idea

Jean-Claude Diels thinks he has a better way to fight lightning. He works in a laboratory at the University of New Mexico. There he makes mini lightning bolts in his lab. Each bolt packs 200,000 volts of electricity.

After creating a lightning bolt, Diels shoots it with a **laser.** A laser makes a concentrated beam of light. In the blink of an eye, the laser blazes a path that lightning can follow. The lightning follows the path to a safe place.

Diels doesn't use an ordinary laser to fight lightning. After all, lightning is fast. It speeds along at 186,000 miles per second. That's the speed of light. Nothing moves faster than light.

So Diels uses a superfast laser. It is called a femtolaser. It flashes in a **femtosecond.** That's a quadrillionth of a second. How does this superfast laser guide lightning through air?

Positive Thinking

To answer that question, we need to find out what makes up air. Air is made of **molecules** of different gases. A molecule is a tiny bit of a substance. Everything is made of molecules.

Laser light gives each air molecule a small **electrical charge.** There are two kinds of electrical charges—positive and negative. The laser gives air molecules a positive charge. Lightning, in contrast, has a negative charge.

The positively charged air molecules attract lightning. The lightning bolt follows the line of charged air molecules created by the laser. The electricity flows to a safe place on the ground.

So far, the laser seems to work in the lab. But will it work in the real world? Diels wants to find out. He plans to place a laser on a truck and then drive into a storm. Diels will shoot laser beams into the thunderclouds. If all goes well, the lasers should guide lightning bolts safely to the ground.

Laser Power

Lasers could eventually be put on top of tall towers and buildings. Laser beams shot into clouds could then attract lightning. That would protect towns and cities from dangerous bolts.

Diels believes that one laser may be able to attract lightning from two miles away. That means only one or two lasers would be needed to protect most communities. That's easier than putting lightning rods on every building. It's also cheaper than shooting lots of rockets into thunderclouds.

Of course, Diels is still working on his laser. He hopes to have a workable system in the near future. "The idea is to be safe from the hazards of lightning," he explained. "Our intention is to create a device that will help protect the public from lightning."

Wordwise

electrical charge: buildup of electricity

femtosecond: quadrillionth of a second

laser: device that makes a concentrated beam of light

meteorologist: scientist who studies weather

molecule: tiny bit of a substance

What Makes Thunder Rumble?

When you see lightning, you often hear thunder. But how does lightning trigger thunder?

Lightning is superhot. A bolt heats the surrounding air to more than 43,000° Fahrenheit. The sizzling heat makes the air expand. After the lightning flashes by, the air cools and contracts. The air moves so quickly that it makes a sound. We call that sound thunder.

Sometimes you may see lightning but not hear thunder. That's because the bolt is very far away. You usually cannot hear thunder made by lightning that's more than ten miles away.

What Makes Lightning?

Lightning flashes when electricity builds up inside a cloud. This happens when wind blows dust particles and water droplets around. The movement creates a positive charge at the top of the cloud. It also forms a negative charge at the bottom.

The ground below a thundercloud has a positive charge. Lightning flashes between areas with opposite charges.

1. The top of a cloud has a positive electrical charge.

2. The bottom of a cloud has a negative electrical charge.

3. The ground has a positive electrical charge.

4. When the positive and negative electrical charges get strong enough, lightning flashes between the cloud and the ground.

5. Lightning also flashes between the top and bottom of a cloud.

© PRECISION GRAPHICS

Kinds of Lightning

Lightning comes in many different forms. Here are a few kinds you might see streak through your neighborhood.

Forked lightning looks like tree branches.

Sheet lightning is a flash of lightning inside a cloud.

Heat lightning is so far away that you cannot hear the thunder it makes.

9

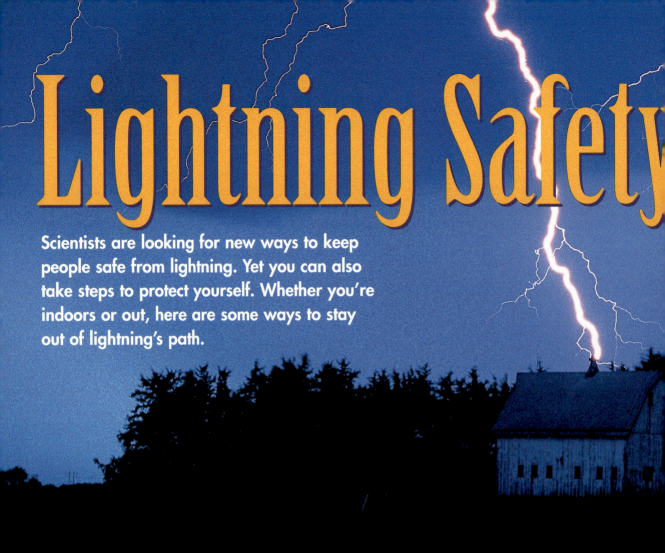

Lightning Safety

Scientists are looking for new ways to keep people safe from lightning. Yet you can also take steps to protect yourself. Whether you're indoors or out, here are some ways to stay out of lightning's path.

Staying Safe Outside

- **Check the weather.** Before you go outside to exercise or play, find out what the weather will be like. Stay home if a bad storm is on its way.

- **Don't fool around.** Lightning is powerful stuff. Don't wait until a storm is on top of you. Go inside at the first sign of thunder or lightning.

- **Find shelter.** Porches and open shelters aren't safe during a storm. Go inside a building. In a pinch, a car will also do.

- **Crouch down.** If you can't find shelter, crouch down as low as you can. Keep your feet together, bend your knees, and tuck your chest to your legs.

- **Stay away from trees.** Standing under a tree might help you stay dry— but it's the last place you want to be in a lightning storm.

- **Avoid metal.** The electricity from lightning can travel along metal fences and poles. During a storm, stay away from any metal objects that you see.

Staying Safe Inside

- **Keep off the porch.** Don't stand on a porch during a storm. Its roof blocks rain, but it doesn't protect you from lightning.

- **Move away from windows.** Glass windows offer no protection from lightning. Stay well inside a room and away from windows.

- **Stay off the phone.** Lightning can travel through phone lines. Wait until after the storm has ended to make a call—or else use a cordless phone.

- **Don't touch cords.** Lightning can travel through electrical wiring into your house. Don't touch plugs or cords during a storm.

- **Wait to wash.** Lightning can travel along water pipes. Don't wash your hands or take a shower during a storm.

- **Wait until the storm ends.** Lightning can strike when you least expect it. Stay indoors for 30 minutes after the last lightning.

Lightning

Answer these shocking questions to find out what you learned.

1 What causes lightning?

2 How often does lightning strike Earth?

3 Explain how a lightning rod works.

4 How might a laser protect people from lightning?

5 Why shouldn't you stand under a tree during a thunderstorm?